IN THE CULINARY WORLD, THERE ARE LOTS OF PATHS TO SUCCESS AND FAILURE—AND A LOT OF UPS AND DOWNS ALONG THE WAY. BUT FEW TRIPS TO THE TOP ARE AS INSPIRING AS THE TRAJECTORY OF YOUNG CHEF DARNELL FERGUSON FROM HIGH SCHOOL CULINARY CLASS TO FOOD NETWORK'S *SUPERCHEF GRUDGE MATCH*. IN THE KITCHEN AND IN LIFE, SUPERCHEF DARNELL HAS NEVER GIVEN UP ON HIMSELF, AND THIS BOOK IS HIS WAY OF BRINGING THE FRUITS OF HIS CULINARY JOURNEY INTO YOUR HOME. CHECK IT OUT!

GUY FIERI

CHEF, RESTAURATEUR, NEW YORK TIMES BESTSELLING AUTHOR, AND EMMY AWARD–WINNING TV HOST

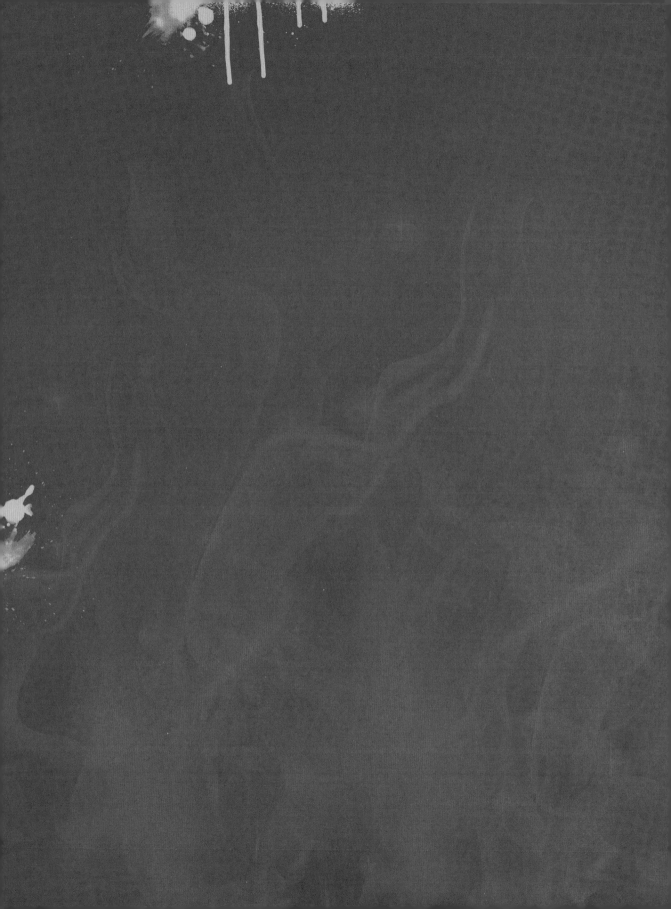

SUPERCHEF FAMILY COOKBOOK

DARNELL FERGUSON

WITH ERIC BENTLEY ★ ILLUSTRATED BY BRAD SMITH

Tyndale House Publishers
Carol Stream, Illinois

Visit Tyndale's website for kids at tyndale.com/kids.

Visit the author's website at iamsuperchef.com.

Tyndale is a registered trademark of Tyndale House Ministries. The Tyndale Kids logo is a trademark of Tyndale House Ministries.

SuperChef Family Cookbook

Designed by Jacqueline L. Nuñez

For manufacturing information regarding this product, please call 1-855-277-9400.

For information about special discounts for bulk purchases, please contact Tyndale House Publishers at csresponse@tyndale.com, or call 1-855-277-9400.

Library of Congress Cataloging-in-Publication Data

A catalog record for this book is available from the Library of Congress.

ISBN 978-1-4964-6228-2

Printed in China

29   28   27   26   25   24   23

7   6   5   4   3   2   1

TO MY WONDERFUL WIFE, TATAHDA; MY AMAZING CHILDREN, DEREON, DALLAS, LOLA, TRINITY, LA'MYA, LEGEND, NELLY, AND NOREI; AND MY NEPHEWS, RZA, MASON, AND JACKSON.

Contents

SNACKS

APPETIZERS AND SIDE DISHES

VEGAN

IT AIN'T EASY BEING SUPER.

This has been my motto for years, but it took me a very long time to realize what it actually meant. But man, when I did, it changed everything. Growing up, I was your normal kid—playing sports, hanging with my friends and family, never really thinking about what the future would hold. When I look back, I believe I always knew I wanted to make a difference in people's lives, and I wanted to change the world. I just didn't know how to find my niche.

I'm a Natural

In my junior year of high school, I went to vocational school for culinary arts. That's where I met Mrs. Cleary. In her culinary class one day, she told us to chop vegetables using different types of cuts that a chef would need to know (julienne, small dice, etc.).

Now, at this point in my life, I had never used any kind of knife besides a basic steak knife at home, and I'd definitely never cooked anything fancy or displayed any interest in the culinary world. So I just went through the motions and didn't think anything of it.

When Mrs. Cleary saw my work, she was in such utter disbelief that I thought I had done something wrong. "Darnell, who taught you how to cut like this?" she asked.

I'VE NEVER DONE THIS BEFORE.

"Mr. Ferguson, this is *unbelievable*! You have the knife skills of someone who has been doing this a very long time. I think you've found your calling."

"YOU'RE A NATURAL!"

I will never forget the feeling that came over me when she said that. It didn't take long before I put my all into the culinary arts. I believed I'd found what I was put on this earth to do, and it's all because someone saw something in me that I didn't see in myself.

Off to College

I was recruited to attend Sullivan University, a college in Louisville, Kentucky, which allowed me to hone my craft. At first, I had a hard time connecting my culture and environment with what I was being taught in school. I didn't even know there were any Black chefs when I started college! In my first year at Sullivan, Chef Demar gave me the first book that I would ever read front to back. The book was about a Black chef with a story similar to mine. He ended up becoming the first Black executive chef in Las Vegas. Reading that book is what inspired me to do the same thing and mark my place in history.

Keep in mind, when I started cooking in the early 2000s, it wasn't the coolest thing to do, and it didn't have the television presence that it has today. I was always a big fan of Emeril Lagasse—how his personality kept an audience engaged and how he really had a passion for what he was cooking. He was one of my first inspirations in the culinary world. Besides Emeril, though, there wasn't anything going on to make me think I'd have exposure and success in cooking.

Olympic Dreams

In 2008, I was one of only twenty-two students in the country selected to cook for Team USA at the Beijing Olympics. What a life-changing opportunity that was! Cooking without recipes for thousands of people a day—many of them with dietary restrictions—was quite a challenge, but I went for it. I wanted to take on as much as I could.

Beijing was when I fully embraced the SuperChef nickname. I have always refused to set limits for myself, and I've always tried taking on more than humanly possible—especially in the kitchen. I had been called SuperChef while cooking at a restaurant in college, but it was said in a mocking way—it wasn't complimentary. I'd just laughed it off then, but I always thought it would be cool to have my own moniker as a chef. So when someone used that nickname for me in Beijing, I wasn't going to let it slip away—I ran with it, and I've been SuperChef ever since!

Lost and Found

When I came back from Beijing, I had a tough time finding my way. I hadn't yet discovered my faith, and I felt like I was on top of the world. I thought I deserved a break since I'd just graduated from college. I tried to take the "easy" way to success and got mixed up in some activities I'm not proud of. As a result, I was in and out of jail seven times. I got kicked out of my apartment and wound up living in my car. Then I crashed at a friend's apartment with eight adults, two pit bulls, and one bedroom. I felt I had nowhere to go and no one to turn to for help.

The last time I was arrested, I realized I could either end up as another statistic or I could turn my life around. I committed to out-working everybody to get where I wanted to be. I thought about the time I'd spent in Beijing: I'd met people there who weren't making livable wages but still appreciated what they had. I knew the bad things I was going through weren't as bad as what others were dealing with, and I taught myself to appreciate my blessings and burdens.

That's when I looked deep in my soul, turned to God, and began exploring my faith. It was time for me to listen to my younger self, the boy who wanted to inspire people and make a difference in their lives. I realized I had made mistakes and needed God's help to make better choices going forward. Ever since, I've fully committed to connecting with people through my food and my faith.

New Beginnings

I started working at a five-star restaurant in Louisville, and I was thriving. I just focused on the task at hand and prepared the food to the best of my ability. I was able to handle and oversee every station of that kitchen, and I understood how to make things run efficiently. One day I took a moment to read the menu, and I couldn't believe what we were charging for some—actually all—of the dishes. I knew how little it cost us to prepare each item, and I told myself I could charge half of that if I started my own restaurant. Plus, I could do things my way and make them even better!

That was when I decided to bet on myself, which has been a recurring theme throughout my life and career. One thing I realized very quickly was how expensive and difficult it was to get started: finding the right location, designing the space, and making sure I had the proper equipment. If I was going to do this, I would have to be creative and would need help. I got together with one of my closest friends from culinary school, and we began to build out our vision.

One day, we were approached by the owner of a local gyro restaurant. It was only open for dinner, so the entire restaurant was sitting empty in the morning and early afternoon. We worked out a deal with the owner to start our own pop-up in his space. This meant we were able to use the restaurant during the hours it wasn't operating. We had to make sure everything was sparkling clean by the time the restaurant staff arrived, and we had to make sure our menu was designed for the hours we were open. It wasn't what I'd dreamed of—I couldn't decorate the way I wanted, and we were constantly under pressure to be in and out on time. However, my faith gave me the strength to keep moving forward, believing in myself, and trusting that God would provide.

This opportunity turned out to be the beginning of something wonderful. Our pop-up had lines out the door every day, and other restaurants throughout the city asked us to open pop-ups in their spaces. We ended up running three different pop-ups at a time, which proved our concept and put us in position to get a loan to open our own restaurant in three years!

My business partner and I spent a lot of time researching different locations, developing the concept and menu, and designing different layouts until we found the perfect place to open our restaurant. We put all our time and energy into creating an atmosphere that would allow people to enjoy a special experience, while also making sure our faith was clear throughout our image. Our motto was "Food, Faith, and Superheroes," and all of our artwork, apparel, and menus shared our message. Business was booming, and we were thrilled—until a few months in, when an electrical fire caused by a faulty air-conditioning system burned the entire restaurant to the ground. For the first time in a while, I felt helpless.

However, as a true testament to my faith, I vowed to keep going. I had an amazing support system within my community, and friends and neighbors were all there to help push me forward. Not too long after, we reopened our restaurant in a new location, thanks be to God.

Into the Spotlight

One day, a local writer interviewed me. During the interview, I thought it was important to include the beginning of my story: how I lost my way, ran into trouble with the law, and lived out of my car— and finally, how I found God, which ultimately saved my life.

Well, let me tell you, once this article made its way to the public, it went viral. All the major daytime talk shows reached out to me, and my social media gained thousands upon thousands of new followers. Before that, I hadn't even thought about competing in any televised cooking competitions. I agreed to go on Rachael Ray's show because I saw it as a calling from God to help inspire others who might be going through struggles like mine.

I was this young, skinny twentysomething kid walking out on national television, and it just felt so natural. Don't get me wrong—I was absolutely nervous, and looking back at the footage, I see how much more comfortable I am in front of a camera now. But I know I gave the audience my authentic self that day. It was truly an amazing experience talking with Rachael on air.

Rachael brought out a surprise guest for me to meet, and I almost passed out from excitement. Out of nowhere, onto the set comes my childhood hero, Emeril Lagasse! I got so emotional. Just being able to shake his hand is something I will never, ever forget. That day, I told myself if I could ever have the type of impact on someone that Emeril had on me, I wouldn't pass it up.

From a young age, I wanted to be great and make a difference, and on that day, I truly believed it was possible. God inspired me to share my story, to make a lasting influence on the lives of people, and to

embrace my flaws as much as my successes. That's why I am writing this book, and I pray that whoever reads it and takes the chance to try out the recipes and techniques will find the same inspiration I did through food and faith.

Super Sanitization and Safety

One of the most important things to learn as you start cooking is how to keep your work area safe and sanitary. These safety measures will help protect you while you're preparing the food—as well as those who will be eating it. Safety starts with preparing your work area, using the right tools, and making sure to properly handle foods that may contain harmful bacteria (meat, fish, eggs, fresh produce, dairy, etc.).

HI! I'M LITTLE SUPER. I'LL BE POPPING UP THROUGHOUT THIS BOOK, SHARING SOME COOKING TRICKS AND WAYS TO MAKE THESE RECIPES EVEN BETTER. LET'S GO!

Keep It Clean

First and foremost, when you're cooking, you should clean as you go. I cannot stress enough the importance of keeping a clean kitchen and workstation, because the more you let the mess pile up, the harder it is to clean and complete your meal. Make sure you have all of your equipment ready to go before you start any recipe. (Each recipe in this book includes a list of the equipment you'll need.) You don't want to be halfway through cooking and then have to scramble to find a strainer or a tool you don't use very often.

A big word you need to always remember (and a big problem you need to avoid) when you're cooking is *cross-contamination*. Cross-contamination is one of the most dangerous risks of the food-preparation process and can cause anyone who eats your food (or who uses the sink after you) to get very sick.

CROSS-CONTAMINATION HAPPENS WHEN BACTERIA OR CONTAMINANTS TRANSFER FROM ONE SURFACE OR SUBSTANCE TO ANOTHER.

Ready-to-eat foods are just that: ready to eat without any preparation or cooking. This includes deli meats, chips, nut mixes, and many vegetables and fruits. Even when you're serving ready-to-eat foods, you need to have a barrier between you and the food, such as gloves, tongs, or utensils. This will eliminate any possible contamination when you're serving these items.

Many other foods require preparation in order to be safe for consumption. This may include heating, removing certain parts, or slicing/cutting. If you're cooking with raw fruit and vegetables, wash them in the sink using a food scrubber before you cut them. It is important to prevent cross-contamination when working with all types of ingredients.

Make sure to wipe down the countertop, cooking surface, or cutting board with a food-safe antibacterial soap before and after use. First, clean it—cleaning will remove any visible contaminants. Then you need to sanitize it—sanitizing will kill the invisible germs on the surface.

Do not use bowls, pans, strainers, cutting boards, or any other pieces of equipment for more than one ingredient unless you wash and sanitize them first. For example, if you're making a chicken dish, use a bowl specifically for the chicken and set it aside from the other ingredients and the cooking surface until you need to use it.

Every time you touch a different food product, wash your hands. I always like to have a few pairs of gloves handy, especially if I'm

YOU CAN NEVER WASH YOUR HANDS ENOUGH!

working with raw meat. I usually use latex gloves, but if you're allergic or prefer to use a plastic glove, go with whatever makes you comfortable. When using gloves to handle raw meat, eggs, or any other product that can cause cross-contamination, make sure you discard the gloves as soon as you're done handling that ingredient and put on fresh ones. (Always use gloves when dealing with raw chicken.) Remember: wash your hands and change your gloves as often as you touch a new ingredient.

Cutting Board Basics

If you're using a cutting board, I suggest putting a damp dish towel underneath so the board doesn't move around while you're cutting. Be sure to examine both sides of the board before you start. Most cutting boards are made for both sides to be used, but sometimes they are curved or have grips or other types of stability supports on the bottom. If you only have one cutting board, make sure you wash it between each ingredient you chop. (Meat should be the last thing you cut on the board.)

Store Things Right

Now we're going to talk a little bit about food storage. Most people don't realize this, but there is a right and a wrong way to store foods in your fridge. The top shelf is for prepared foods and fruits and vegetables (unless your fridge has a separate drawer or compartment for these items). Under that goes smaller dairy products, and under that goes pork, beef, seafood, and chicken. Make sure to keep the different types of meat apart from one another on the bottom shelf. Eggs and milk go in the bottom compartment of the door. Depending on the size of your fridge, it may not be possible to space everything out like

this. The main thing to remember is to keep produce, raw meats, and dairy separate from each other.

Track the Temperature

Another safety requirement to keep in mind—especially when cooking meat—is the temperature.

 Scan this QR code for a demonstration of how to measure the temperature of meat with a cooking thermometer.

Here is a list of safe cooking temperatures to keep handy in the kitchen:

COOKING TEMPS LIST

TYPE OF FOOD	MINIMUM TEMPERATURE
Fish	145°F (65°C)
Ham	145°F (65°C)
Beef and Pork	145°F (65°C)
Ground Beef and Pork	160°F (70°C)
Chicken and Turkey	165°F (75°C)
Ground Chicken and Turkey	165°F (75°C)

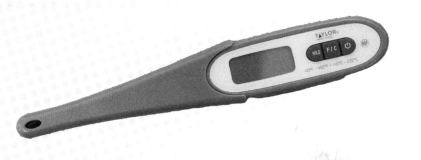

WHEN YOU NEED TO CHECK THE TEMPERATURE OF THE MEAT OR WHATEVER YOU'RE COOKING, THE BEST WAY TO MEASURE IT IS BY INSERTING A COOKING THERMOMETER INTO THE THICKEST PART OF THE MEAT OR WHATEVER YOU'RE COOKING.

Make sure you remove the food from the oven first. Measuring the temperature while food is in the oven could cause a burn or other injury, as well as an inaccurate reading.

Once the food reaches the desired temperature, it will continue cooking after it's removed from the stove or oven. It's important to let meat rest for at least 3–5 minutes before you cut into it. If you don't, the juices will leak out, and that will impact the taste.

Tools and Techniques for the SuperChef in Training

SUPERHEROES ARE THE VERY BEST AT WHAT THEY DO.

Sometimes it comes naturally, and sometimes it takes a lot of practice and experience for them to fully understand their powers. Batman wasn't born a superhero, but years of learning martial arts and acquiring the necessary resources enabled him to become one. This section covers the skills you need so you can be comfortable working in the kitchen. The recipes in this cookbook feature some of these techniques.

Knife Essentials

If you want to be super in the kitchen, skill with a knife is one of the first abilities you'll need.

> **WHEN YOU USE A KNIFE, MAKE SURE TO FOLLOW THESE IMPORTANT SAFETY PRECAUTIONS:**

- Do not cut on a wobbly or slippery cutting board.

- Make sure you have a good grip on the knife handle and keep your fingers away from the blade.

- Tuck your fingers while holding whatever item you're cutting.

SCAN THE QR CODES THROUGHOUT THIS BOOK FOR A FIRSTHAND LESSON FROM SUPERCHEF HIMSELF!

When you're first learning how to work with knives, there are several basic, classic cuts you need to master.

Peel: remove skin or rind with a peeler

Mince: finely chop foods into tiny pieces

Chiffonade: a fancy term for slicing leafy greens or vegetables, such as basil; roll up the herbs or leafy lettuce/greens and slice them finely.

Julienne: matchstick-size cuts for fruits or vegetables

Small dice: ¼-inch (1 cm) square-shaped cut

Medium dice: ½-inch (1.5 cm) square-shaped cut

Large dice: ¾-inch (2 cm) square-shaped cut

 Scan this QR code to see a demonstration of how to properly make each cut.

IF YOU USE YOUR KNIFE THE RIGHT WAY, YOU'LL BE A CUT ABOVE!

Professional chefs use many types of knives. When you're first starting out in the kitchen, though, you should practice with safer and more manageable knives like these:

Dog knife: sharp enough to cut through produce, but not sharp enough to pierce your skin

Chef's knife: a versatile knife that can be used for all basic cuts. Use this for cutting proteins, such as meats and tofu. Adult supervision is highly recommended when using this knife. I suggest an 8-inch blade for beginners.

Paring knife: a smaller knife used for fine cuts on larger items

Serrated bread knife: a long, saw-like blade used to cut bread

Useful Utensils

The recipes in this book require you to measure the ingredients. You'll need a standard set of measuring cups and spoons (or a measuring cup with ml marks if you're measuring in milliliters). Most sets include 1 cup, ½ cup, ⅓ cup, ¼ cup, 1 tablespoon, 1 teaspoon, ½ teaspoon, and ¼ teaspoon. If you're measuring in grams, make sure to have a food scale on hand.

Many of the recipes also require other utensils and equipment. Here's a list of some of the most important tools you'll need:

Whisk: a cooking utensil with a long handle and a series of wire loops. This is used for whisking or whipping to incorporate air into a mixture.

Spatula: a broad, flat, flexible utensil used to spread, mix, and lift foods

Wooden spoon: often used for cooking on the stovetop because they don't transfer as much heat as metal utensils

Baking dish: an oven-safe container mainly used for baking casseroles or pasta dishes

IT'S IMPORTANT TO GET OUT ALL THE TOOLS AND EQUIPMENT YOU'LL NEED BEFORE YOU START A RECIPE. BE PREPARED!

Mixing bowls: various-sized bowls for mixing ingredients before or after cooking

Oven mitts: safety gloves that allow you to properly and safely handle hot items

Skewers: long sticks (made of wood or metal) used to pierce and hold several small items at once to assist in cooking and turning

Pots and Pans 101

Think of pots and pans as the vehicles of the dishes you make. Here are some of the most common pots and pans you'll need for the recipes in this book.

Stockpot: a large pot with a thick base, often used to cook soup

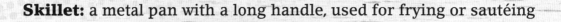

Skillet: a metal pan with a long handle, used for frying or sautéing

Saucepan: a small but deep pot with a long handle, used to cook sauces and other liquids

Saucepot: a larger version of the saucepan with taller sides

Roasting pan: a large, deep pan with handles, used for cooking meat and vegetables in the oven

Sheet pan: a thin, shallow pan, used for baking in the oven

Sauté pan: a pan with high, straight sides and a lid

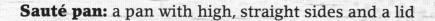

MAKE SURE TO PREHEAT POTS AND PANS BEFORE PUTTING INGREDIENTS IN THEM! STARTING WITH A COLD SURFACE CAN RESULT IN UNEVEN COOKING.

Cooking Methods

Chefs need to know a lot of different terms that describe all the ways food can be cooked. These are a few of the key terms to learn as you start your cooking adventure.

Roasting: cooking with high heat in an oven or over a fire

Baking: heating food in an oven with hot, dry air at a lower temperature than roasting

Frying: cooking food in a skillet with hot fat or oil

Sautéing: heating food quickly in a little hot fat or oil

Searing: cooking at a high temperature until a crust forms on the surface of the food

Boiling: raising the temperature of liquid until it bubbles

 Scan this QR code to see the difference between frying and sautéing.

WHEN YOU'RE WORKING WITH HOT EQUIPMENT AND LIQUIDS, KEEP THE SURROUNDING AREAS UNCLUTTERED.

USE SILICONE OR HEAT-RESISTANT GLOVES— NEVER TOUCH HOT ITEMS WITH YOUR BARE HANDS.

OUCH!

I HAVE A PRETTY BIG FAMILY—ME, MY WIFE, AND OUR EIGHT KIDS—AND THERE'S ALWAYS SOMETHING GOING ON AT OUR HOUSE.

Everyone's a little different, which is very obvious in the mornings. Some of us like to sleep in as late as we can, and others are out of bed first thing. But at least one morning a week, we all get up at the same time to share breakfast.

Spending time together as a family helps us appreciate one another and show everyone some love. It's an incredible way to start the day. You'll be able to start a breakfast tradition in your own home with the SuperChef recipes in this chapter!

Breakfast

DONUT PANCAKES
(SERVES 5)

PANCAKE INGREDIENTS

- ½ cup (120 ml) distilled vinegar
- 2⅓ cups (560 ml) milk
- 2 large eggs
- 1 tablespoon (15 ml) vanilla extract or paste
- 4 cups (560 g) all-purpose flour
- 1 cup (200 g) granulated sugar
- 2 tablespoons (30 ml) baking powder
- 1 tablespoon (15 ml) baking soda
- Nonstick cooking spray

ICING INGREDIENTS

- 8 ounces (225 g) cream cheese (softened)
- 1½ cups (105 g) whipped topping
- ½ cup (60 g) powdered sugar
- Red food coloring
- Rainbow sprinkles

EQUIPMENT

- 2 large mixing bowls
- Whisk
- Sifter
- Ladle or large spoon
- Flattop griddle
- Spatula
- Toothpicks
- Circle-shaped cookie cutters in large (about 3–4 inch [8–10 cm] diameter) and small (about 1 inch [3 cm] diameter) sizes
- Cutting board
- Hand mixer with whisk attachment

INSTRUCTIONS

1. Combine vinegar and milk in a mixing bowl. Do not stir. Let sit for 5 minutes.

2. In a separate bowl, sift all the dry ingredients (flour, sugar, baking powder, baking soda) together.

3. Add eggs and vanilla to the vinegar-milk mixture and whisk together.

 Scan this QR code to see two methods for cracking an egg.

4. Combine the wet ingredients with the dry ingredients and whisk together.

 Scan this QR code to see how to use a whisk.

COMBINING THE VINEGAR AND MILK IS MY VERY OWN TRIED AND TRUE WAY TO MAKE BUTTERMILK. WATCH CLOSELY WHEN YOU COMBINE THEM—YOU SHOULD SEE AN INSTANT TRANSFORMATION!

5. Preheat the flattop griddle to 350°F (180°C) and spray with the nonstick cooking spray.

6. Using about ⅓ cup (80 ml) batter per pancake, ladle batter in several different locations on the griddle until it is full.

7. Cook pancakes until bubbles begin to form on top (approximately 3 minutes), then flip with the spatula and cook until golden brown (approximately 2 more minutes).

    FLIPPING PANCAKES CAN BE TRICKY! MAKE SURE YOU HAVE AN ADULT AROUND TO GIVE YOU SOME HELP IF YOU NEED IT.

8. Remove the cooked pancakes from the griddle to cool. Repeat the cooking process with the rest of the pancake batter until it's all gone.

    TO MAKE SURE THE PANCAKES ARE COOKED THROUGH, POKE A TOOTHPICK INTO THE CENTER, THEN REMOVE. IF THE TOOTHPICK COMES OUT CLEAN, THE PANCAKES ARE DONE; IF THERE'S BATTER ON THE TOOTHPICK, COOK A LITTLE LONGER.

9. Make the icing by first using the hand mixer with its whisk attachment to cream the cream cheese in a bowl until no lumps remain. Add the whipped topping and powdered sugar and mix until combined. Add a couple drops of food coloring and mix, then add more if needed until the icing is pink.

10. Once your pancakes are cool, cut them into neat circles with the large cookie cutter. Then use the small cookie cutter to cut a hole in the middle of each so they look like donuts!

11. Spread the icing on the donut pancakes and top with sprinkles!

GREEN WAFFLES
(SERVES 5)

INGREDIENTS

- ½ cup (120 ml) distilled vinegar
- 2 cups (480 ml) milk
- 2 large eggs
- 1 tablespoon (15 ml) vanilla extract or paste
- ¼ cup (60 ml) green food coloring (preferred brand: Gordon Choice)
- 4 cups (560 g) all-purpose flour
- 1½ cups (300 g) granulated sugar
- 2 tablespoons (30 ml) baking powder
- 1 tablespoon (15 ml) baking soda
- Nonstick cooking spray
- Powdered sugar

EQUIPMENT

- 2 mixing bowls
- Whisk
- Sifter
- Ladle or large spoon
- Waffle iron

IF YOU DON'T HAVE A WAFFLE IRON, NO PROBLEM! YOU CAN USE THIS RECIPE TO MAKE GREEN PANCAKES INSTEAD.

INSTRUCTIONS

1. Combine vinegar and milk in a mixing bowl. Do not stir. Let sit for 5 minutes.

2. In a separate bowl, sift all the dry ingredients (flour, sugar, baking powder, baking soda) together.

3. Add eggs and vanilla to the vinegar-milk mixture and whisk together. Add a few drops of food coloring and mix, then add more if needed until the mixture is dark green.

4. Combine the wet ingredients with the dry ingredients and whisk together.

5. Turn on waffle iron and set heat to low. Spray with the nonstick cooking spray.

 Scan this QR code for a demonstration of how to use a waffle iron.

BE SURE TO READ YOUR WAFFLE IRON'S INSTRUCTIONS BEFORE YOU OPERATE IT!

6. Ladle the batter into one side of the waffle iron, close the lid, and flip. Remove the waffle when it's finished and place on a plate or tray to cool. Repeat the process with the rest of the waffle batter until it's all gone.

7. Dust powdered sugar on the finished waffles.

FRENCH TOAST CUPCAKES
(MAKES 8 CUPCAKES)

INGREDIENTS

- 4 large eggs
- 1½ cups (360 ml) milk
- 1 tablespoon (15 ml) cinnamon
- ½ teaspoon (2.5 ml) nutmeg
- 1 tablespoon (15 ml) vanilla extract or paste
- 1½ teaspoons (7.5 ml) orange extract (or orange zest)
- ½ cup (120 ml) maple syrup
- Nonstick cooking spray
- 8 slices of white bread (You can also be creative and try your favorite bread!)
- Spray bottle of whipped topping
- 10 strawberries (sliced)
- 2 cups (300 g) blueberries
- 1 cup (200 g) mandarin orange segments (drained)
- Powdered sugar
- Sprinkles

EQUIPMENT

- Cupcake/muffin tin
- Whisk
- Mixing bowl
- Piping bag (optional)

INSTRUCTIONS

1. Preheat the oven to 400°F (205°C).

2. Mix eggs, milk, cinnamon, nutmeg, vanilla, orange extract, and maple syrup with the whisk.

3. Grease the cupcake tin with nonstick cooking spray.

4. Dip both sides of each slice of bread in the egg mixture, then place in the cupcake tin. Be sure to press the 4 corners of the bread together to get it into the tin.

5. Once all slices of bread are dipped and in the cupcake tin, place in oven and cook for 8–14 minutes. If you like softer French toast, cook for a shorter time. If you want it firmer, cook a little longer.

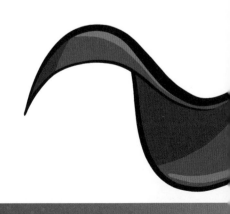

6. Once cooked to your liking, remove from oven and let set for 5 minutes.

7. Spray whipped topping in the middle of each French toast cupcake. (You can also make your own whipped cream and pipe it into the French toast using a piping bag.)

8. Top each cupcake with the fruit, and finish with powdered sugar and sprinkles as desired.

EGG MUFFINS
(MAKES 12 MUFFINS)

INGREDIENTS

- 1 pack refrigerated biscuits (6–8 count, optional)
- 8 large eggs
- 1 cup (240 ml) milk
- 2 tablespoons (30 ml) garlic and herb seasoning
- ½ cup (60 g) shredded cheddar cheese
- ½ cup (60 g) shredded Parmesan cheese
- ½ cup (150 g) roasted red peppers (small diced)
- 1 cup (60 g) fresh spinach (chopped and packed tightly)
- 1 cup (80 g) turkey bacon (cooked and small diced)
- Nonstick cooking spray

EQUIPMENT

- Sheet pan (if you're baking the biscuits)
- Mixing bowl
- Whisk
- Mixing spoon
- Ladle or large spoon
- Cupcake/muffin tin
- Table knife

USE YOUR IMAGINATION WHEN YOU'RE COOKING! TRY ADDING YOUR FAVORITE INGREDIENTS TO THESE EGG MUFFINS INSTEAD OF THE ONES LISTED HERE. YOU CAN CHOOSE YOUR OWN SPICES, CHEESES, VEGETABLES, PROTEIN, AND EVEN YOUR OWN TYPE OF BISCUITS!

INSTRUCTIONS

1. Cook the biscuits in advance by following the package instructions (optional).

2. Preheat the oven to 350°F (180°C).

3. Whisk eggs and milk in the mixing bowl, then add all other ingredients and mix.

4. Spray cupcake/muffin tin with nonstick cooking spray and ladle the egg mixture into the molds, filling them ¾ of the way to the top.

5. Cook for 15–20 minutes. They're ready to take out when you insert a knife into a muffin and it comes out clean. Remove from oven and let cool for 10 minutes.

6. Run a knife around the edges of the egg muffins, then remove them from the mold.

7. If you want to make a breakfast sandwich, place an egg muffin between two biscuit halves!

PB & J OATMEAL

(SERVES 2)

OATMEAL INGREDIENTS

- 4 cups (960 ml) milk
- 1 cup (150 g) quick-cook steel-cut oats
- 1 cup (240 g) peanut butter
- ½ cup (170 g) pure maple syrup

BLUEBERRY JELLY SAUCE INGREDIENTS

- 6 ounces (170 g) blueberries (plus extra for topping)
- 1 cup (240 ml) water
- ½ cup (100 g) brown sugar (or coconut sugar)

EQUIPMENT

- Medium saucepot
- Whisk
- Medium saucepan
- Blender
- Serving bowl

I LIKE USING PURE MAPLE SYRUP BECAUSE IT'S A NATURAL PRODUCT WITH NO HIGH-FRUCTOSE CORN SYRUP.

65

INSTRUCTIONS

1. Warm milk in saucepot on medium heat until it simmers.

2. Add oats and whisk. You will need to consistently stir the oatmeal about every minute until it's done. (Follow the directions on the package of oats to see how long they need to cook.)

3. After about 5 minutes, add the peanut butter and maple syrup to the pot and continue cooking. The oatmeal mixture will thicken while you make the blueberry jelly sauce in the next step.

4. Heat blueberries in medium saucepan with water and sugar at a low temperature until the liquid is reduced by half.

5. Pour blueberry mixture into blender, and blend until smooth.

 Scan this QR code to learn how to use a blender.

HOLD DOWN THE LID OF THE BLENDER WITH YOUR HAND. THE HOT LIQUID WILL CAUSE PRESSURE TO BUILD, AND IF YOU AREN'T HOLDING THE LID, YOU WILL HAVE A BIG MESS TO CLEAN UP.

FOR A FUN VARIATION, LEAVE OUT THE BLUEBERRY JELLY SAUCE. TOP THE OATMEAL WITH CHOCOLATE CHIPS INSTEAD FOR A DELICIOUS PEANUT BUTTER CUP OATMEAL. YUM!

6. Pour the blended mixture back into the saucepan and cook on medium-low for 5 minutes to finish the blueberry jelly sauce.

7. Scoop the oatmeal into a serving bowl and drizzle it with the blueberry jelly sauce. Top with fresh blueberries (as desired).

Lunch

Some people call lunch the forgotten meal, but it's important to make sure you eat it! When I was a kid, I cared more about running outside for recess than sitting and eating my lunch. Maybe you can relate! As I got older, I found other reasons to skip lunch: too busy at work, needing to be somewhere and not enough time to eat, filming a show and needing to learn my lines.

A few years ago, I decided to make sure I eat lunch every day, no matter how busy I am. This decision has no doubt changed my life for the better. I have so much more energy to do everything I need to do, I get less tired and cranky, I don't hit that "wall" in the middle of the day, and my body and mind are in the best shape of my life.

GOD ONLY GIVES US ONE BODY. IT'S OUR JOB TO CARE FOR IT AND MAKE SURE WE DON'T TAKE IT FOR GRANTED.
BE SURE TO GIVE YOURSELF THE FUEL YOU NEED BY MAKING TIME FOR A HEALTHY LUNCH. THIS SECTION WILL GIVE YOU SOME GREAT LUNCH IDEAS TO SHARE WITH FRIENDS AND FAMILY!

SUPER SMASH BURGERS
(SERVES 8)

BURGER INGREDIENTS

- 2 pounds (900 g) ground beef
- 2 tablespoons (30 ml) minced garlic
- 2 tablespoons (30 ml) steak or BBQ sauce
- ½ tablespoon (7.5 ml) kosher salt
- 2 tablespoons (30 ml) ground black pepper
- 8 slices American or cheddar cheese
- Hamburger buns (split)

SAUCE INGREDIENTS

- ½ cup (120 g) ketchup
- ½ cup (120 g) garlic aioli
- 2 tablespoons (30 ml) sweet relish
- 1 tablespoon (15 ml) honey mustard
- 1 teaspoon (5 ml) smoked paprika

EQUIPMENT

- Flattop griddle
- 2 mixing bowls
- Spatula
- Whisk
- Cooking thermometer
- Serving tray

AFTER MAKING THESE BURGERS, YOU'LL NEVER WANT TO BUY ANOTHER FROZEN OR PREMADE BURGER PATTY AGAIN!

1. Preheat flattop griddle.

2. Mix beef, garlic, steak or BBQ sauce, salt, and pepper together in mixing bowl.

3. Portion the beef mixture into 4-ounce (110 g) patties and spread them out on the flattop griddle. Use the spatula to smash down the meat.

4. Cook the patties for 3 minutes, then flip them over.

5. Top each patty with cheese and cook for an additional 3 minutes. Check the temperature by inserting the cooking thermometer into the center of a patty. Once the meat has reached an internal temperature of 160°F (70°C), remove the patties from the griddle and place on the serving tray.

6. Toast the buns on the flattop griddle split side down.

7. Make the sauce: combine all ingredients in a mixing bowl. Whisk until completely mixed.

8. Spread the sauce on the bun. Put the burger in the bun and enjoy!

PB & J SUSHI CRUNCH

(SERVES 1)

INGREDIENTS

- 4 slices white bread
- 2 tablespoons (30 ml) peanut butter
- 2 tablespoons (30 ml) grape or strawberry jelly
- 2 tablespoons (30 ml) roasted peanuts
- 2 tablespoons (30 ml) blueberries

EQUIPMENT

- Cutting board
- Rolling pin
- Table knife
- Chef's knife or mallet
- Ziplock bag

IF YOU DON'T HAVE A ROLLING PIN, YOU CAN GET CREATIVE AND USE A SODA BOTTLE. JUST DON'T SHAKE THE BOTTLE OF SODA!

INSTRUCTIONS

1. Cut crust off each slice of bread. Roll each slice thin using the rolling pin.

 Scan this QR code to see how to use a rolling pin.

2. Spread a thin layer of peanut butter on two slices of bread. Spread a thin layer of jelly on the other two slices.

3. Finely chop peanuts using a chef's knife. (You can also place them in a ziplock bag and use a mallet to pound them.) Sprinkle the peanuts on the slices with peanut butter.

4. Layer the rolled-out bread slices by placing a jelly slice on top of a peanut butter slice, a peanut butter slice on top of that jelly slice, then the last jelly slice on top of the peanut butter slice.

5. Roll the combined slices tightly, doing your best to keep them from bunching up, until you have what looks like a log.

6. Slice the roll into 5–6 pieces. Garnish with any remaining chopped nuts and the blueberries.

YOU CAN ROAST YOUR OWN PEANUTS BY MIXING 1 POUND (450 G) OF PEANUTS WITH 2 TABLESPOONS (30 ML) OF MELTED BUTTER AND 1/3 CUP (100 G) OF HONEY.

DEEP-DISH PIZZA TOAST

(SERVES 6)

INGREDIENTS

- Nonstick cooking spray
- 6 slices Texas toast (garlic-flavored, defrosted)
- 2 cups (480 g) pizza sauce
- 1 cup (120 g) shredded mozzarella cheese
- Sliced pepperoni
- Fresh basil
- Any other favorite pizza toppings

EQUIPMENT

- Oven with broiler
- Sheet pan
- Ladle or spoon

INSTRUCTIONS

1. Preheat oven to 400°F (205°C). Grease the sheet pan with nonstick cooking spray.

2. Use your fingers to flatten each slice of bread, starting from the center and working outward until you reach the crust. Put them on the sheet pan.

3. Toast in oven for 2 minutes (until very lightly browned). Remove from oven.

4. Ladle or spoon a layer of sauce on each slice, followed by cheese, pepperoni, basil, and any other toppings.

5. Switch oven to low broiler setting.

6. Place the sheet pan on the bottom rack and broil until cheese is melted. Let cool before eating.

IF YOU WANT TO MAKE YOUR OWN TEXAS TOAST, THE KEY IS TO USE A NICE PIECE OF THICK BREAD (ABOUT ¾ INCH TO 1 INCH [2 TO 3 CM] THICK). FOR THE 6 SLICES OF TEXAS TOAST THIS RECIPE CALLS FOR, MELT 1 STICK (120 G) OF UNSALTED BUTTER AND COMBINE WITH 2 TABLESPOONS (30 ML) OF MINCED GARLIC, 1 TEASPOON (5 ML) OF GARLIC POWDER, 1 TABLESPOON (15 ML) OF DRIED PARSLEY, AND 1 TEASPOON (5 ML) OF KOSHER SALT.

MIX THE BUTTER, GARLIC, GARLIC POWDER, DRIED PARSLEY, AND SALT. SPREAD THE MIXTURE ON THE SLICES OF BREAD, THEN PLACE THE BREAD ON A GREASED SHEET PAN AND BAKE FOR ABOUT 12 MINUTES (FLIPPING THEM HALFWAY THROUGH) UNTIL GOLDEN BROWN ON EACH SIDE.

ULTIMATE GRILLED CHEESE

(SERVES 1)

INGREDIENTS

- 4 cups (480 g) shredded mozzarella cheese
- 1 tablespoon (15 ml) red food dye
- 1 tablespoon (15 ml) blue food dye
- 4 teaspoons (20 ml) mayonnaise
- 3 slices potato bread
- 4 tablespoons (60 ml) Boursin cheese (garlic and fine herbs flavor)
- 2 slices white American or cheddar cheese
- 2 tablespoons (30 ml) honey for drizzling

EQUIPMENT

- Flattop griddle
- 2 mixing bowls
- Mixing spoon
- Table knife
- Spatula

DON'T WORRY IF YOU'VE NEVER HEARD OF BOURSIN CHEESE! IT'S BASICALLY JUST A SUPER FLAVORFUL CREAM CHEESE WITH DIFFERENT HERBS AND SPICES. WANT TO MAKE YOUR OWN? TAKE 16 OUNCES (450 G) OF CREAM CHEESE AND 1 STICK OF UNSALTED BUTTER (120 G), THEN LET THEM SOFTEN AT ROOM TEMPERATURE.

COMBINE IN A MIXING BOWL AND ADD ½ CUP (60 G) GRATED PARMESAN, ¼ CUP (60 G) MINCED GARLIC, AND 1½ TEASPOONS (7.5 ML) EACH OF ANY OR ALL OF THE FOLLOWING: BLACK PEPPER, DRIED MARJORAM, BASIL, CHIVES, PARSLEY, DRIED THYME, AND KOSHER SALT.

1. Preheat flattop griddle to 400°F (205°C).

2. Place ½ cup (60 g) mozzarella cheese in a bowl with the red food dye and mix well.

3. Place the rest of the mozzarella cheese in a separate bowl with the blue food dye and mix well.

4. Spread mayonnaise on one side of each slice of bread.

5. Spread 2 tablespoons (30 ml) of Boursin cheese on 1 piece of bread (the side with no mayonnaise).

6. Place a slice of American cheese on each piece of bread that doesn't have Boursin on it.

7. Put dyed cheese on the 2 pieces of bread that have the American cheese on them. Place red and blue cheese side by side until the bread is covered.

8. Carefully put all 3 slices of bread on the griddle (mayonnaise side down).

9. Once the cheese is melted and the bread is toasted, use the spatula to close the three layers of the sandwich and enjoy. (If the cheese isn't melting, put the sandwich in the oven at 400°F [205°C] for a few minutes.)

10. Cut in half and drizzle with honey.

I LOVE GRILLED CHEESE! IT'S SO VERSATILE, AND YOU CAN MAKE IT SOOOO MANY DIFFERENT WAYS. YOU CAN TAKE THIS RECIPE AND SUBSTITUTE YOUR FAVORITE BREAD AND CHEESES—AND ADD ANY TOPPINGS YOU WANT.

PHILLY CHEESESTEAK HOT POCKETS

(SERVES 4)

INGREDIENTS

- 2 sheets puff pastry
- All-purpose flour
- 16 ounces (450 g) precooked Philly steak (small diced)
- 4 tablespoons (60 ml) steak sauce
- 4 tablespoons (60 ml) Alfredo sauce
- ½ cup (100 g) caramelized onions
- 1 cup (120 g) shredded mozzarella cheese
- 1 cup (120 g) shredded smoked Gouda cheese
- 1 large egg
- 2 tablespoons (30 ml) water

EQUIPMENT

- Table knife
- Rolling pin
- Sheet pan
- Parchment paper
- Small bowl
- Whisk
- Basting brush

THE KEY TO BAKING WITH PUFF PASTRY IS TO KEEP IT COLD AND NOT LET IT GET TO ROOM TEMPERATURE, BECAUSE THEN THE BUTTER WILL SOFTEN AND THE DOUGH WILL GET ALL STICKY AND DIFFICULT TO WORK WITH. DON'T TAKE THE PUFF PASTRY OUT OF THE FRIDGE UNTIL YOU ARE 100 PERCENT READY TO WORK WITH IT!

INSTRUCTIONS

1. Preheat oven to 425°F (220°C).

2. Sprinkle flour on the counter so the dough doesn't stick. Lay out the puff pastry sheets and divide each into quarters with a knife.

3. Sprinkle the tops of each quarter with flour. Dust the rolling pin with flour and use it to flatten each puff pastry sheet separately.

4. Place ¼ cup of steak (56 g) on one half of each puff pastry quarter.

5. Drizzle the steak sauce and the Alfredo sauce over the meat, using 1½ teaspoons (7.5 ml) of each per pastry sheet square.

6. Divide the onions among the pastry sheet squares.

7. Sprinkle the mozzarella and Gouda cheeses on top of the other ingredients, using 2 tablespoons (30 ml) of each per pastry sheet square.

8. Fold each puff pastry square over and press a fork around the edges to ensure nothing leaks when cooked. Trim off any excess pastry if needed.

9. Line the sheet pan with parchment paper and place the pastry pockets on the pan.

10. Crack the egg in a small bowl and whisk with 2 tablespoons (30 ml) of water to make an egg wash. Brush the egg wash on the puff pastry (just enough to cover—you don't need to use it all).

11. Cook until golden brown.

Dinner

One of my favorite things to do is cook dinner for my family and friends and eat together. Going out for meals is nice, but it can be pricey, and there's just this special feeling you get watching your loved ones enjoy a meal you prepared.

Every now and then, think of a friend and their family to cook for and share a meal with. Ask your parent or guardian for permission and invite this family over for a meal. Maybe even ask your friend to come over early and help you cook one of the recipes in this book! One of the amazing things about food is how it can help bring joy and build stronger relationships with people in your life!

SIT AT THE DINNER TABLE AND SAY A PRAYER OF THANKS FOR THE FOOD YOU'RE ABOUT TO EAT AND THE PEOPLE YOU'RE SHARING IT WITH —THEN DIG IN!

CHICKEN AND VEGGIE KEBABS
(SERVES 5)

MARINADE INGREDIENTS

- 2 cups (480 ml) soy sauce or liquid aminos
- ½ cup (100 g) dark brown sugar (or maple brown sugar)
- ½ teaspoon (2.5 ml) paprika
- ½ teaspoon (2.5 ml) garlic powder
- 1 teaspoon (5 ml) sesame oil

KEBAB INGREDIENTS

- 1 pound (450 g) boneless, skinless chicken breasts
- 1 large red bell pepper
- 1 large yellow bell pepper
- 15 button mushrooms
- 3 tablespoons (45 ml) olive oil
- Salt and pepper
- 1 bunch cilantro
- ½ cup (140 g) Korean BBQ sauce

YOU CAN USE CAULIFLOWER OR TOFU INSTEAD OF CHICKEN IF YOU'RE LOOKING FOR A VEGETARIAN OPTION.

EQUIPMENT

- 2 mixing bowls
- Whisk
- Ziplock bag
- Chef's knife
- Cutting board
- 5 metal skewers
- Sheet pan
- Parchment paper
- Oven with broiler
- Cooking thermometer

IF YOU DON'T HAVE METAL SKEWERS, YOU CAN USE WOOD SKEWERS INSTEAD. JUST MAKE SURE YOU SOAK THEM IN WATER FOR AT LEAST AN HOUR BEFORE COOKING SO THEY DON'T BURN.

INSTRUCTIONS

Day before serving:

1. In a mixing bowl, create the marinade: whisk together the soy sauce or liquid aminos, brown sugar, paprika, garlic, and sesame oil.

2. Place chicken in the ziplock bag, add the marinade, and refrigerate overnight.

Next day:

1. Preheat oven to 400°F (205°C). Take chicken out of refrigerator and drain marinade.

2. Cut the peppers into 1-inch (3 cm) chunks. Cut off the bottoms of the mushrooms, discard, and rinse the tops.

3. Cut the chicken breasts into 1-inch (3 cm) chunks.

4. In a mixing bowl, toss all the vegetables in the olive oil and season with salt and pepper.

 Scan this QR code for a demonstration of how to apply seasoning.

5. Skewer the chicken and veggies, alternating chicken, peppers, mushrooms, chicken, etc.

6. Place kebabs on a sheet pan covered with parchment paper.

7. Cook in the oven for 15 minutes, rotating the kebabs every 5–6 minutes. Then move the pan under the broiler, turn the broiler to high, and cook for an additional 4–6 minutes (until the internal temperature of the chicken is 165°F [75°C]).

8. Rinse and chop cilantro.

9. Garnish the kebabs with cilantro and a drizzle of Korean BBQ sauce.

IF YOU DON'T HAVE KOREAN BBQ SAUCE, YOU CAN PICK ANY BBQ SAUCE YOU LIKE.

LITTLE SUPER'S LASAGNA
(SERVES 8)

INGREDIENTS

- 3 tablespoons (45 ml) olive oil
- 1 white onion (small diced)
- 4 tablespoons (60 ml) minced garlic
- 1 pound (450 g) ground beef
- 1 pound (450 g) ground sausage
- Salt and pepper
- 8 cups (960 g) tomato sauce
- 5 tablespoons (75 ml) brown sugar
- 2 cups (480 g) ricotta cheese
- 1 cup (120 g) grated Parmesan cheese
- ½ cup (30 g) fresh parsley (finely chopped)
- Nonstick cooking spray
- 1 12-ounce (340 g) box of oven-ready lasagna noodles
- 2 cups (480 g) Alfredo sauce
- 4 cups (480 g) shredded mozzarella cheese
- 1½ cups (180 g) shredded Parmesan cheese

EQUIPMENT

- Sauté pan (medium)
- Spatula
- Mixing bowl
- Whisk
- Large baking dish
- Aluminum foil

IF YOU WANT TO REALLY IMPRESS, MAKE YOUR OWN ALFREDO SAUCE! PLACE A SKILLET ON THE STOVETOP AND TURN TO LOW HEAT. ADD ½ STICK (60 G) BUTTER AND 1½ CUPS (360 ML) HEAVY CREAM AND LET SIMMER FOR ABOUT 2 MINUTES, STIRRING OCCASIONALLY.

WHISK IN 2 TABLESPOONS (30 ML) MINCED GARLIC, ½ TEASPOON (2.5 ML) ITALIAN SEASONING, AND SALT AND PEPPER TO TASTE. THEN WHISK IN 2 CUPS (240 G) GRATED PARMESAN UNTIL THE CHEESE IS MELTED, AND SERVE!

INSTRUCTIONS

1. Preheat oven to 350°F (180°C).

2. Place sauté pan on stove at medium heat. Let pan get hot (about 1 minute).

3. Add 3 tablespoons (45 ml) of olive oil to the pan. Then add the onion and sauté for about 3 minutes.

4. Add 2 tablespoons (30 ml) of the minced garlic and sauté for another minute.

5. Add the ground beef and sausage and cook until meat is browned. (Break up, but don't stir too frequently.) Drain if needed.

6. Season with salt and pepper.

7. Add tomato sauce and brown sugar, cook for another 5 minutes, and set aside.

8. In a mixing bowl, add ricotta, grated Parmesan, the remaining minced garlic, and parsley. Whisk until fully combined.

9. Grease the baking dish with nonstick cooking spray, then begin to layer the lasagna into the dish in the following order:

    a. approximately 1 cup (240 g) meat sauce on bottom of dish
    b. 3 lasagna noodles
    c. another 1½ cup (360 g) layer of meat sauce
    d. approximately 2 cups (240 g) shredded mozzarella (spread out evenly)
    e. another layer of lasagna noodles
    f. approximately 1 cup (240 g) Alfredo sauce (spread out evenly)
    g. approximately 1 cup (240 g) of the ricotta cheese mixture (spread out evenly)
    h. 1 cup (120 g) shredded Parmesan cheese (spread out evenly)
    i. another layer of lasagna noodles

10. Finish by placing the following ingredients on the final layer of noodles: 2 cups (480 g) meat sauce, the rest of the ricotta cheese mixture, ½ cup (60 g) Parmesan, and 2 cups (240 g) of mozzarella.

11. Cover the dish with aluminum foil, place in oven, and bake for 40 minutes.

12. Remove foil and place the dish on the bottom rack. Turn oven to a low broil and cook until golden brown (about 7–10 minutes).

13. Let rest for 15 minutes before cutting.

TUESDAY TACOS
(SERVES 8)

SAUCE/MARINADE INGREDIENTS

- 2 cups (480 ml) soy sauce or liquid aminos
- ½ cup (120 ml) rice vinegar
- ¼ cup (50 g) granulated sugar
- ½ cup (100 g) brown sugar
- 2 tablespoons (30 ml) sesame oil
- ½ cup (120 g) minced garlic
- 2 tablespoons (30 ml) fresh ginger (peeled and grated)
- 5 scallions (finely chopped)

TACO INGREDIENTS

- 1½ pounds (675 g) steak (flank, flat iron, or sirloin)
- 16 street taco tortillas
- 1 white onion (small diced)
- 1 bunch cilantro (rough chopped)

EQUIPMENT

- Mixing bowl
- Mixing spoon
- Small saucepot
- Cutting board
- Ziplock bag
- Chef's knife
- Flattop griddle
- Medium bowl
- Taco holders (optional)

> MAKE THE MARINADE THE DAY BEFORE SO THE MEAT HAS TIME TO SOAK IN THE FLAVORS YOU CREATED—AND THEY WON'T BE LOST IN THE COOKING PROCESS. THE MARINADE ALSO TENDERIZES THE MEAT AND MAKES IT COOK MORE EASILY.

INSTRUCTIONS

Day before serving:

1. In mixing bowl, combine soy sauce or liquid aminos, rice vinegar, granulated sugar, brown sugar, sesame oil, minced garlic, ginger, and scallions.

2. Put half of this mixture in a small saucepot. Heat on stove at medium and simmer until the mixture is reduced by half. (This will be the sauce that goes on your tacos.) Let the sauce cool, then transfer to a glass container to store in refrigerator.

3. Place the remaining uncooked mixture in the ziplock bag. Finely slice the steak and add to the marinade.

4. Refrigerate the sauce and the steak overnight.

Next day:

1. Turn flattop griddle to 450°F (230°C).

2. Remove marinated steak from refrigerator and drain marinade.

3. Place tortillas on griddle for approximately 10 seconds on each side, just until warm.

4. Cook steak on top of griddle for approximately 3 minutes on each side. Set aside in a bowl until all the steak is cooked. Once steak is cooked and cooled, cut into smaller pieces.

5. Assemble the tacos by laying out tortillas (or putting them in taco holders). Add steak, sauce (from day before), onion, and cilantro.

BACON FRIED RICE

(SERVES 4)

INGREDIENTS

- 4 slices of bacon (cut into small pieces before cooking)
- 1 cup (225 g) white onion (small diced)
- 1 cup (225 g) carrot (grated)
- 1 tablespoon (15 ml) olive oil
- 4 cups (1000 g) cooked rice (brown, jasmine, or basmati; day-old rice is best to use)
- 2 large eggs
- ½ cup (120 ml) soy sauce or liquid aminos
- ½ cup (120 g) sweet chili sauce

EQUIPMENT

- Large sauté pan or wok
- Spatula

INSTRUCTIONS

1. Put sauté pan on medium heat for about 1 minute (let pan get hot).

2. Add bacon and cook for about 3 minutes until brown without burning.

3. Add onion and combine with the bacon. Cook until softened.

4. Add carrot. Sauté for another minute.

5. Add olive oil and rice. Sauté for about 2 minutes.

6. Create a well: push the rice to the sides of the pan so there is a circular opening in the middle. Add the eggs to the well and stir them in the middle until they are cooked.

7. Once eggs are done, stir everything together. Add soy sauce or liquid aminos and sweet chili sauce. Mix for another minute or two.

IF YOU'RE NOT A FAN OF BACON, USE GROUND PORK SAUSAGE INSTEAD.

HONEY-BAKED TURKEY

(SERVES 4-6)

GLAZE INGREDIENTS

- ½ cup (100 g) brown sugar
- 1 cup (200 g) granulated sugar
- ½ teaspoon (2.5 ml) onion powder
- ½ teaspoon (2.5 ml) cinnamon
- ½ teaspoon (2.5 ml) nutmeg
- ¼ teaspoon (1.25 ml) ginger
- ¼ teaspoon (1.25 ml) paprika
- ½ cup (120 ml) water

TURKEY INGREDIENTS

- ½ cup (120 ml) olive oil
- 4 tablespoons (60 ml) minced garlic
- 1 tablespoon (15 ml) Cajun seasoning
- 1 tablespoon (15 ml) Italian seasoning
- 3 pounds (1350 g) turkey breast with skin on

ITALIAN SEASONING IS BASICALLY A BLEND OF DRIED HERBS—OREGANO, MARJORAM, THYME, BASIL, ROSEMARY, AND SAGE. YOU CAN MAKE YOUR OWN OR BUY IT AT THE STORE.

- Small saucepot
- Whisk
- Small mixing bowl
- Basting brush
- Sheet pan or roasting pan
- Aluminum foil
- Cooking thermometer

INSTRUCTIONS

1. Preheat oven to 400°F (205°C).

2. Add all ingredients for glaze to a saucepot on the stovetop, cooking at medium heat. Whisk until glaze comes to a boil, then turn off heat and set aside.

3. In a small mixing bowl, combine oil, garlic, Cajun seasoning, and Italian seasoning to make a marinade. Rub over the turkey breast, including under the turkey skin.

4. Place turkey breast on the sheet pan or roasting pan, and cover it loosely with aluminum foil in the shape of a tent. Roast in oven for 1 hour.

LET'S GET STARTED!

5. Remove foil and brush on the glaze with the basting brush. Put turkey back in oven. Glaze every 15 minutes until turkey is cooked (about 30 more minutes).

6. Remove turkey from oven. Place the cooking thermometer in the center of the thickest part of the turkey. Make sure it reads 165°F (75°C) or higher. If it's not there yet, return the turkey to the oven for an additional 20 minutes. Then check again.

7. When the turkey is fully cooked, remove it from oven and brush on excess glaze as desired.

THE BREAST IS THE LEANEST PART OF ANY POULTRY DISH (TURKEY, CHICKEN, ETC.), WHICH MEANS IT HAS LITTLE TO NO FAT AND CAN EASILY DRY OUT. COVERING THE PAN WITH ALUMINUM FOIL HELPS KEEP THE MEAT FROM GETTING DRY.

STICKY AIR-FRIED CHICKEN
(SERVES 4)

GLAZE INGREDIENTS

- 2 cups (680 g) pure maple syrup
- 1 cup (200 g) brown sugar
- 1 cup (240 ml) hot sauce (pick a heat you can tolerate)
- 3 tablespoons (45 ml) cornstarch
- 3 tablespoons (45 ml) cold water

CHICKEN INGREDIENTS

- 2 tablespoons (30 ml) olive oil
- 2 teaspoons (10 ml) Cajun seasoning
- 2 teaspoons (10 ml) BBQ seasoning
- 4 pounds (1800 g) chicken wings

EQUIPMENT

- Small saucepot
- Whisk
- Small mixing bowl
- Fork
- Air fryer
- 2 large mixing bowls
- Mixing spoon
- Cooking thermometer

IF YOU DON'T HAVE AN AIR FRYER, PUT THE WINGS ON A SHEET PAN AND USE THE CONVECTION SETTING ON YOUR OVEN TO COOK THEM. PREHEAT YOUR OVEN TO 450°F (230°C) AND COOK FOR 25 MINUTES. FLIP THE WINGS, THEN COOK FOR ANOTHER 25 MINUTES.

INSTRUCTIONS

1. Prepare glaze by whisking maple syrup, brown sugar, and hot sauce in a small saucepot. Place on stove at medium heat. Bring to a simmer.

2. Combine cornstarch and cold water (using a fork) in a very small mixing bowl, then whisk into the glaze.

3. Continue whisking until the glaze comes to a boil, then turn off heat.

4. Preheat air fryer to 400°F (205°C).

5. In a large mixing bowl, combine the olive oil, Cajun seasoning, and BBQ seasoning. Rub the mixture all over each of the wings.

6. Layer the wings in the air fryer. (Make sure they are not touching.) Cook for 10 minutes.

7. Flip the wings and cook for another 6–10 minutes until they are browned. Place the cooking thermometer in one of the larger wings. Make sure it reads 165°F (75°C) or higher.

8. Transfer wings to a clean mixing bowl. Toss them with the glaze, then serve.

SCIENCE IS A BIG PART OF COOKING! WHISKING CORNSTARCH INTO THE GLAZE CAUSES A CHEMICAL REACTION THAT ENABLES IT TO THICKEN AND STICK BETTER TO THE WINGS.

WITH ASPARAGUS AND ROASTED POTATOES
(SERVES 4)

SALMON

GLAZE INGREDIENTS

- 1½ cups (360 ml) orange juice
- 1 cup (340 g) honey
- 4 tablespoons (60 ml) minced garlic
- 1 tablespoon (15ml) water
- 1 tablespoon (15ml) cornstarch

SALMON INGREDIENTS

- 4 6-ounce (170 g each; 680 g total) salmon filets
- BBQ seasoning
- Nonstick cooking spray
- 4 tablespoons (60 ml) olive oil

EQUIPMENT

- Small saucepot
- Whisk
- Small mixing bowl
- Flattop griddle
- Sheet pan
- Spatula

INSTRUCTIONS

1. Make the glaze by combining orange juice, honey, and garlic in a small saucepot and stirring with a whisk.

2. In a small mixing bowl, mix the water and cornstarch. Set aside.

3. Cook the glaze on medium until mixture is reduced by half.

4. Add the water-cornstarch mixture to the glaze and whisk on the stove until it reaches desired thickness (about 1–2 minutes).

5. Season the salmon with BBQ seasoning, as desired.

6. Turn the flattop griddle to 450°F (230°C) and wait about a minute or two for it to fully heat.

7. Add 1 tablespoon (15 ml) of olive oil in 4 separate spots on the cooking surface of the griddle.

8. Place 1 filet on top of each oiled section. Cook for 4 minutes on one side.

9. While the filets are cooking, preheat oven to 425°F (220°C) and grease the sheet pan with nonstick cooking spray.

10. Carefully flip filets with the spatula.

11. As you cook the other sides of the filets, use a spoon to drizzle some of the glaze on the sides that have already been cooked.

12. After 4 additional minutes of cooking, transfer the filets to the greased sheet pan. Bake in the oven for 8 minutes.

13. Remove the fish from the oven and add the remaining glaze (as desired).

ASPARAGUS

INGREDIENTS

- 1 bunch asparagus
- 2 tablespoons (30 ml) extra virgin olive oil
- Salt and pepper
- 1 teaspoon (5 ml) lemon zest
- 1 Parmesan wedge (or ¼ cup [30 g] grated Parmesan)

EQUIPMENT

- Flattop griddle
- Chef's knife
- Cutting board
- Mixing bowl
- Tongs
- Serving tray
- Cheese grater (if using Parmesan wedge)

INSTRUCTIONS

1. Preheat flattop griddle to 450°F (230°C).

2. Rinse the asparagus, then break or cut off the white bottoms and discard.

3. Place asparagus in mixing bowl, toss with olive oil, and season with salt and pepper.

4. Lay asparagus on griddle, turning periodically with tongs. Cook for 5–8 minutes, depending on thickness. (Thicker pieces need to cook longer. Thinner pieces will cook in a shorter amount of time.) Finished asparagus should show some char marks and still have a slight crunch.

5. Place asparagus on serving tray and sprinkle with lemon zest and grated cheese.

POTATOES

INGREDIENTS

- 3 pounds (1350 g) Yukon Gold potatoes (cut into ½ inch [1.5 cm] pieces)
- Cold water
- ½ teaspoon (2.5 ml) baking soda
- Nonstick cooking spray
- ½ cup (120 ml) olive oil
- 3 tablespoons (45 ml) minced garlic
- 3 tablespoons (45 ml) fresh thyme (remove leaves from stems)
- Salt and pepper

EQUIPMENT

- Stockpot
- Strainer
- Sheet pan
- Mixing bowl
- Mixing spoon
- Spatula

INSTRUCTIONS

1. Preheat oven to 425°F (220°C).

2. Place potatoes in the stockpot and add cold water until they are fully covered.

3. Add baking soda to the water and place on stove at high heat.

4. Once the water comes to a boil, cook for 10 minutes.

5. Drain the water using the strainer and let potatoes dry completely.

6. Grease sheet pan with cooking spray.

7. Place the potatoes in the mixing bowl, and toss with olive oil, garlic, thyme, salt, and pepper (as desired). Spread out potatoes on the greased sheet pan (make sure they aren't on top of each other).

8. Roast in oven for 15 minutes. Remove briefly to flip the potatoes using a spatula, then roast for another 10–15 minutes.

ONE OF THE PURPOSES OF THIS BOOK IS TO PREPARE YOU TO COOK MORE COMPLEX MEALS, BUT YOU HAVE TO CRAWL BEFORE YOU CAN WALK! TAKE YOUR TIME AND LEARN AT YOUR OWN PACE. THAT'S HOW YOU'LL BECOME A MASTER OF YOUR CRAFT.

Snacks

If you play sports, or go running around with friends, or ride your bike, or if you just wake up early one day, you need to make sure you're giving your body all it needs to function well.

These snacks are healthier options that you can enjoy instead of candy or chips, which are high in fat and sugar. When you try these recipes, you'll see how wholesome, natural ingredients can taste delicious and keep you full and energized. Make these snacks for when you have a movie night with a group of friends, or bring them to a ball game and eat them on the sidelines with your teammates to help give you that extra push!

SOMETIMES YOUR REGULAR MEALS DON'T FEEL LIKE ENOUGH TO GIVE YOU ALL THE ENERGY YOU NEED!

APPLE NACHOS
(SERVES 2)

INGREDIENTS

- 1 apple
- 2 tablespoons (30 ml) lemon juice mixed with 2 cups (480 ml) water
- ¼ cup (60 g) peanut butter sauce (or microwaved peanut butter)
- 8 large pretzel sticks
- ¼ cup (60 g) chocolate chips
- 2 tablespoons (30 ml) shredded coconut
- ¼ teaspoon (1.25 ml) cinnamon
- ¼ cup (40 g) peanuts
- 1 chopped-up Heath bar

EQUIPMENT

- Chef's knife
- Cutting board
- Large plate

1. Wash and dry apples. Cut them into quarters and remove the seeds and stems.

2. Cut the quarters into thin slices. Soak the slices in the lemon juice–water mixture for 3–5 minutes to keep them from turning brown. Remove slices from water and dry, then place them in the bowl.

3. Spread the apple slices across the plate. Cover them with the toppings so they resemble nachos (with the apples serving as the nacho chips).

MAKE THESE NACHOS YOUR OWN! THERE ARE SO MANY TOPPINGS YOU CAN USE THAT I DIDN'T EVEN MENTION ABOVE. TRY YOUR FAVORITE CHOCOLATE BAR INSTEAD OF A HEATH BAR, ALONG WITH SOME HEALTHY ALTERNATIVES.

GRANOLA
(SERVES 6-8)

GRANOLA INGREDIENTS

- ½ cup (120 ml) canola oil
- ½ cup (170 g) honey or maple syrup
- ½ teaspoon (2.5 ml) kosher salt
- 1 tablespoon (15 ml) peanut butter powder
- 1 teaspoon (5 ml) cinnamon
- 3 cups (240 g) old-fashioned rolled oats
- 1 cup (90 g) sliced or slivered almonds

TOPPINGS

- Sliced strawberries
- Blueberries

IF YOU DON'T HAVE PEANUT BUTTER POWDER, TRY PEANUT BUTTER CHIPS INSTEAD. ADD THEM AFTER BAKING WITH THE OTHER TOPPINGS.

EQUIPMENT

- 2 mixing bowls
- Whisk
- Wooden spoon
- Parchment paper
- Sheet pan
- Spatula

INSTRUCTIONS

1. Preheat oven to 300°F (150°C).

2. In a mixing bowl, whisk canola oil, honey or maple syrup, salt, peanut butter powder, and cinnamon.

3. Add oats and almonds and stir everything with a wooden spoon until fully combined.

4. Spread evenly on the parchment paper–covered sheet pan.

5. Bake for 30 minutes, then remove from oven to turn the mixture with the spatula so the wet parts are on top. Bake another 30 minutes until golden brown. (The mixture may still be a little wet when you remove it from the oven, but it will dry.)

6. Let the mix cool. Scrape the cool, dry mixture into a clean mixing bowl and break it up with a spoon.

7. Top the granola with fruit and enjoy.

MIX VARIOUS TOPPINGS SUCH AS MARSHMALLOWS, CHOCOLATE CHIPS, AND RAISINS INTO YOUR GRANOLA TO MAKE A TRAIL MIX. IT ALSO MAKES A GREAT TOPPING ON ICE CREAM OR YOUR FAVORITE YOGURT!

RANCH POPCORN

(SERVES 4-6)

INGREDIENTS

- 1 bag microwavable low-fat popcorn
- 2 tablespoons (30 ml) ranch seasoning
- 1 tablespoon (15 ml) table salt
- 2 tablespoons (30 ml) grated Parmesan cheese
- 2 tablespoons (30 ml) chives (dried or finely chopped)

EQUIPMENT

- Microwave
- Serving bowl
- Small mixing bowl

INSTRUCTIONS

1. Microwave popcorn according to instructions.

2. Toss 1 tablespoon of ranch seasoning over popcorn in serving bowl.

3. Mix Parmesan cheese with remaining tablespoon of ranch dressing in the second small mixing bowl. Sprinkle over popcorn (leave about 1 tablespoon [15 ml] remaining).

4. Combine the remaining cheese blend with the chives, and dust it over the popcorn.

BBQ POPCORN

(SERVES 4-6)

INGREDIENTS

- 1 bag microwavable low-fat popcorn
- 1 tablespoon (15 ml) sweet BBQ seasoning
- 2 cups (120 g) BBQ-flavored chips

EQUIPMENT

- Microwave
- Serving bowl

INSTRUCTIONS

1. Microwave popcorn according to instructions.

2. Toss sweet BBQ seasoning over popcorn in serving bowl.

3. Toss 1 cup (60 g) of the BBQ-flavored chips with the popcorn, and mix well.

4. Top off with remaining 1 cup (60 g) of BBQ-flavored chips.

THERE ARE SO MANY OPTIONS WITH POPCORN!

DRIZZLE MELTED CHOCOLATE OVER YOUR POPCORN, OR ADD YOUR FAVORITE CARAMEL FOR THE SALTY/SWEET ELEMENT.

GO SAVORY BY ADDING YOUR FAVORITE SPICES!
OR YOU CAN REALLY GET CREATIVE BY PICKING DIFFERENT MEALS OR DESSERTS AND TRYING TO REPLICATE THEM INTO POPCORN FLAVORS!

FRUIT PIZZAS WITH SUGAR COOKIE CRUST

(SERVES 6–8)

CRUST INGREDIENTS

- Nonstick cooking spray
- 1 package refrigerated sugar cookie dough balls
- 2 cups (160 g) whipped cream cheese (room temperature)
- 1½ cups (105 g) whipped topping (room temperature)
- 1 cup (120 g) powdered sugar
- 1 tablespoon (15 ml) vanilla extract or paste

TOPPINGS

- 1 kiwi (peeled and sliced thin)
- 1 8.5 ounce (240 g) can mandarin oranges (drained)
- 10 strawberries (sliced thin)
- 1 cup blueberries
- 10 red grapes (sliced in half)
- 10 green grapes (sliced in half)

EQUIPMENT

- 12-inch (30 cm) pizza pan
- Mixing bowl
- Hand mixer with whisk attachment (or whisk)
- Spatula for spreading

NO PIZZA PAN IN YOUR KITCHEN? YOU CAN USE ANY FLAT PAN! JUST LEAVE SPACE AROUND THE EDGES FOR THE DOUGH TO EXPAND.

1. Preheat oven to 350°F (180°C).

2. Spray 12-inch (30 cm) pizza pan with nonstick cooking spray.

3. Place sugar cookie dough balls evenly around the pizza pan, leaving about ½ inch (1.5 cm) of space around the edges. Press them down with light pressure to make more room for your toppings.

4. Bake until golden brown (10–12 minutes). Remove from oven and let cool completely.

5. In a mixing bowl, combine cream cheese, whipped topping, powdered sugar, and vanilla. Use hand mixer with whisk attachment (or a whisk) to mix until no lumps remain.

6. Use the spatula to spread a thin layer of the cream cheese mixture on the cookies once they're cool.

7. Arrange fruit on cookies, layering in a circular design.

WHEN YOU MAKE THIS DISH, THINK OF YOURSELF AS AN ARTIST. FIND A BALANCE IN THE SHAPES AND COLORS OF THE FRUIT, AND MAKE SURE EVERY SLICE OF PIZZA GETS A LITTLE BIT OF EVERYTHING.

ACAI SMOOTHIES
(SERVES 4)

INGREDIENTS

- 2 cups (300 g) frozen strawberries
- 2 cups (300 g) bananas (sliced thin, then frozen)
- ¾ cup (170 g) vanilla yogurt (or your favorite flavor)
- 1 3½-ounce package (100 g) frozen acai
- 2 tablespoons (30 ml) orange juice

TOPPINGS

- Granola
- Sliced strawberries
- Blueberries
- Chia seeds
- Shredded coconut
- Honey

EQUIPMENT

- Blender

INSTRUCTIONS

1. Put frozen strawberries, bananas, yogurt, acai, and orange juice in a blender and mix well. (Do not overblend, or it will become watery.)

2. Pour into a bowl and add toppings as desired.

I LOVE FROZEN ACAI BECAUSE IT'S A SUPERFRUIT! I LIKE TO BREAK IT INTO SMALLER PIECES BEFORE I PUT IT IN THE BLENDER SO IT BLENDS MORE EASILY. YOUR SMOOTHIE SHOULD BE THICK ENOUGH TO EAT WITH A SPOON. IF YOU NEED TO MAKE IT THICKER, TRY ADDING MORE FROZEN FRUIT.

Appetizers and Side Dishes

Whether you're part of a sports team, an orchestra, a group project, or anything else that requires working with others, you may have heard the saying "Teamwork makes the dream work!" You can be the best player on the team, but if you can't cooperate with your teammates, you're probably not going to succeed. The same goes for food: you can make the best lasagna, but if you can't pair it with some good sides or a delicious appetizer, the meal will feel like something's missing.

So far, we have worked on a bunch of recipes that can be the star, and now it's time to build a supporting cast that makes the meal complete! These sides are easy to make, great to accompany a main dish, and delicious options to bring if you're eating at someone else's home.

SPINACH-ARTICHOKE DIP
(SERVES 8–10)

INGREDIENTS

- 8 ounces (225 g) low-fat cream cheese (softened)
- 8 ounces (240 g) low-fat sour cream
- 5 strips reduced-sodium bacon
- 14.5 ounce jar (425 g) marinated artichoke hearts (small diced)
- 2 roasted red peppers, sliced thin
- 4 cups (225 g) fresh spinach
- 1 cup (120 g) grated Parmesan
- Chopped herbs, such as chives and parsley, for garnish

EQUIPMENT

- Mixing bowl
- Cutting board
- Chef's knife
- Sauté pan with lid
- Spatula
- Hand mixer
- Slotted spoon
- Sheet pan lined with paper towels
- Serving bowl

1. Place cream cheese and sour cream in mixing bowl.

2. Place sauté pan on stove on medium heat and let it get hot (about 1–2 minutes).

3. Place diced bacon in pan and let cook, allowing the fat to render (melt down).

4. Once bacon is approaching crispy (about 6–8 minutes), add diced artichokes and red peppers, stirring occasionally for two minutes.

5. Lower heat on pan and sprinkle spinach on top. Cover pan and cook until spinach begins to shrink.

6. While waiting for spinach to cook, use a hand mixer to combine the cream cheese and sour cream.

7. Stir the spinach-artichoke mixture. Once it's cooked through, remove from pan with a slotted spoon if there's excess fat. Place the mixture on the sheet pan lined with the paper towels to remove the rest of the fat. Pour the remaining bacon fat into the empty artichoke jar and allow to cool before discarding.

8. Add the spinach-artichoke mixture, the cream cheese–sour cream mixture, and the Parmesan back to the pan and heat for 5–6 minutes until the cheese is melted.

9. Be sure to taste and see if anything else is needed, such as salt or additional cheese. Sprinkle chopped herbs on top and enjoy.

MAC & CHEESE

(SERVES 10–12)

INGREDIENTS

- 6 strips bacon (optional)
- 3 tablespoons (45 ml) brown sugar (if making bacon)
- 2 tablespoons (30 ml) jerk seasoning (if making bacon)
- 16 ounces (450 g) cavatappi pasta
- 1 stick (120 g) butter
- ½ cup (70 g) all-purpose flour
- 6 cups (1440 ml) heavy cream
- 2 cups (240 g) shredded sharp cheddar cheese
- ¾ cup (90 g) shredded smoked Gouda cheese
- 7 slices (140 g) pepper jack cheese
- 2½ tablespoons (37.5 ml) garlic salt
- 1½ tablespoons (22.5 ml) onion powder
- 1 tablespoon (15 ml) Cajun seasoning
- 1 tablespoon (15 ml) kosher salt
- 2 tablespoons (30 ml) fresh cracked black pepper
- Nonstick cooking spray

EQUIPMENT

- Sheet pan
- Large stockpot
- Strainer
- Large saucepan
- Sifter
- Medium mixing bowl
- Wooden spoon
- Whisk
- Large mixing bowl
- Large baking dish (cast iron preferred)

INSTRUCTIONS

1. Preheat oven to 400°F (205°C).

2. Line slices of bacon on sheet pan and bake in oven until bacon is about 75% cooked (around 7–10 minutes).

3. Remove from oven, sprinkle with brown sugar and jerk seasoning, then place back into oven until fully cooked (about 5 minutes). Leave the oven on.

4. While bacon is cooling, cook pasta in stockpot per instructions on the box. Strain once cooked and set aside.

5. Dice bacon and set aside.

6. Sift flour into a mixing bowl.

7. Place saucepan on stove and set to medium-low heat. Heat butter until melted, then add sifted flour and stir with wooden spoon.

8. Cook for about 2 minutes, then whisk in heavy cream, bringing it to a simmer. Add half of all cheeses, all remaining seasonings, and most of the bacon (whisk until fully incorporated). Set aside a little bacon to use as a topping.

9. Add cooked pasta to a large mixing bowl. Add the cheese sauce and mix with a wooden spoon, then add remaining Gouda and pepper jack.

10. Spray the baking dish with nonstick cooking spray and pour the mac & cheese into the dish.

11. Top with the remaining cheddar and bake for 30 minutes until top is brown and macaroni is bubbling.

12. Sprinkle the remaining crushed-up bacon on top and enjoy!

THE THREE TYPES OF CHEESE IN THIS RECIPE MAKE AN AWESOME TEAM! CHEDDAR HAS A SHARP, STRONG FLAVOR. SMOKED GOUDA IS SMOKY AND CREAMY. AND PEPPER JACK GIVES A NICE KICK.

PASTA SALAD

(SERVES 10–12)

INGREDIENTS

- 16 ounces (450 g) pasta (choose your preferred kind)
- 1 cup (150 g) cherry tomatoes (sliced in half)
- 1 cup (225 g) red onion (julienned)
- ½ bunch asparagus (large dice after cutting three inches off the bottom)
- 1 cucumber (medium dice)
- 1 yellow bell pepper (julienned)
- 1 tablespoon (15 ml) minced garlic
- ¼ cup (7.5 g) cilantro (finely chopped)
- 3 cups (720 ml) roasted red pepper Italian dressing
- 1½ cups (180 g) shredded Parmesan cheese

EQUIPMENT

- Large stockpot
- Strainer
- Mixing bowl
- Mixing spoon
- Serving bowl

INSTRUCTIONS

1. Cook pasta per instructions on the box. Strain and set aside to cool to room temperature.

2. Meanwhile, prepare the vegetables according to the ingredients list.

3. In a large mixing bowl, mix cooled pasta, vegetables, Italian dressing, and 1 cup (120 g) shredded Parmesan cheese.

4. Place in a serving bowl and sprinkle the remaining Parmesan on top.

IT'S VERY IMPORTANT TO LET THE PASTA COOL BEFORE YOU ADD THE OTHER INGREDIENTS. HOT OR WARM PASTA WILL SOFTEN THE OTHER INGREDIENTS AND MESS UP SOME OF THE TEXTURES THAT MAKE THIS SALAD SPECIAL.

STREET CORN LOLLIPOPS
(SERVES 6)

INGREDIENTS

- 6 6-inch (15 cm) pieces of corn on the cob
- 1 12-ounce (360 g) bottle of garlic aioli
- 1 cup (120 g) cotija cheese (crumbled; or use grated Parmesan)
- ½ bunch cilantro (finely chopped)
- 2 tablespoons (30 ml) paprika

EQUIPMENT

- 6 wood skewers (soaked in water for 24 hours, then removed and dried)
- Stockpot
- Strainer
- Large plate
- Serving plate

INSTRUCTIONS

1. Boil water in stockpot.

2. Cook corn in boiling water for 5–7 minutes. Strain, let cool, and place a skewer through the center of each corn cob.

3. Roll the corn in the aioli on a large plate. Then, sprinkle with the cotija cheese or grated Parmesan and the cilantro, and dust with the paprika as desired.

4. Place each completed piece of corn on a serving plate.

IF YOU DON'T HAVE GARLIC AIOLI, YOU CAN JUST COMBINE 3/4 CUP (180 ML) STORE-BOUGHT MAYONNAISE AND 1/2 TEASPOON (2.5 ML) GARLIC POWDER.

TWICE-COOKED POTATOES

(SERVES 4–6)

INGREDIENTS

- 3 large Idaho potatoes (washed and dried)
- 1 tablespoon (15 ml) vegetable oil
- Salt and pepper
- 2 tablespoons (30 ml) heavy cream or milk
- ½ cup (120 g) shredded cheddar cheese, plus a little extra for topping
- 2 tablespoons (30 ml) Boursin cheese (garlic and fine herbs flavor)
- 2 tablespoons (30 ml) minced garlic
- 2 egg yolks
- 2 tablespoons (30 ml) fresh chives (chopped)
- ½ tablespoon (7.5 ml) Cajun seasoning
- ½ tablespoon (7.5 ml) Italian seasoning

EQUIPMENT

- Fork
- Microwave-safe plate
- Chef's knife
- Cutting board
- Mixing bowl
- Spoon or scoop
- Whisk
- Piping bag with large star tip
- Oven with broiler
- Sheet pan

IF YOU DON'T HAVE A PIPING BAG, JUST PUT THE MASHED POTATO MIXTURE IN A BOWL AND USE A SPOON TO TRANSFER IT TO THE POTATO SKINS.

INSTRUCTIONS

1. Preheat oven to 400°F (205°C).

2. Drizzle oil on whole potatoes, use a fork to poke holes, then add a pinch of salt and pepper.

3. Place potatoes on microwave-safe plate. Bake for 17 minutes, turning over halfway through.

4. Let potatoes cool until you can comfortably touch them without getting burned, then cut them in half longways.

5. Scoop out the center of each potato, and place whatever you scoop out in a mixing bowl. (There should be about ¼ inch [1 cm] of potato left on both sides of the potato skin once you've scooped everything out.)

6. Add heavy cream or milk, both cheeses, garlic, egg yolks, seasonings, and chives to the potato mixture. Whisk until everything is mixed together.

7. Set oven on broil at high heat.

8. Place mashed potato mixture in piping bag. Pipe two potato towers inside each potato skin and top with remaining cheese.

9. Transfer potatoes to sheet pan. Bake under broiler until lightly browned (5–8 minutes).

Vegan

One thing I learned early in my cooking career is that what tastes good to me won't necessarily taste good to someone else. Many people have food allergies, and many others eat according to a vegan or vegetarian diet. People who follow a vegan diet generally won't eat anything that comes from a living being (meat, milk, eggs, etc.). A vegetarian diet isn't as strict as a vegan one. Vegetarians refrain from eating meat and, sometimes, meat products.

When you're cooking for other people, it's a good idea to ask them ahead of time if they have any dietary restrictions. The recipes in this section are creative and tasty options that anyone will love, even if they're not vegan or vegetarian!

OATMEAL PANCAKES

(SERVES 4–6)

INGREDIENTS

- 3 cups (240 g) old-fashioned oats
- 1 banana (overripe with some brown spots)
- ¼ cup (30 g) vanilla protein powder (or your preferred vegan protein powder)
- 1 tablespoon (15 ml) vanilla extract or paste
- ¼ teaspoon (1.25 ml) cinnamon
- 1 cup (240 ml) vanilla almond milk
- 3 tablespoons (45 ml) stevia
- Nonstick cooking spray

TOPPINGS

- Blueberries and sliced strawberries
- Honey or maple syrup

USING A BANANA THAT'S OVERRIPE GIVES THESE PANCAKES EXTRA FLAVOR AND SWEETNESS.

EQUIPMENT

- Flattop griddle
- Bullet blender (or regular blender)
- Ladle or large spoon
- Spatula
- Circle-shaped cookie cutter in large size (about 3–4 inch [8–10 cm] diameter)
- Cutting board

INSTRUCTIONS

1. Preheat griddle to 400°F (205°C).

2. Combine all ingredients in blender and blend until fully combined. Be careful not to overblend, since the batter should have the texture of oatmeal.

3. Spray griddle with nonstick cooking spray.

4. Ladle pancake mix onto griddle in about ¼ cup (60 ml) amounts. Cook for 2 minutes, then flip and cook for another 2 minutes.

5. Once your pancakes are cool, cut them into neat circles with the large cookie cutter. Add toppings as desired.

VEGAN SLOPPY JOES

(SERVES 4–6)

INGREDIENTS

- 1 pound (450 g) Impossible meat (or other plant-based meat)
- 3 tablespoons (45 ml) minced garlic
- 1 tablespoon (15 ml) kosher salt
- 1 teaspoon (5 ml) fresh cracked black pepper
- ½ cup (120 ml) steak sauce
- 2 tablespoons (30 ml) olive oil
- 1 onion (small diced)
- 3 cups (720 ml) BBQ sauce
- Hamburger buns (slightly toasted in 400°F [205°C] oven for 2 minutes)

EQUIPMENT

- Mixing bowl
- Mixing spoon
- Large sauté pan
- Spatula

THERE ARE SO MANY DIFFERENT BRANDS OF PLANT-BASED MEAT! EXPLORE THE DIFFERENT TYPES AND FIND THE ONE YOU LIKE BEST.

1. Combine Impossible meat, garlic, salt, pepper, and steak sauce in mixing bowl.

2. Place sauté pan on the stove at medium heat for 1 minute.

3. Put olive oil in the sauté pan, and sauté onions in the oil for about 5 minutes.

4. Add the Impossible meat to the pan and continue to cook for about 6 minutes, occasionally mixing until the meat is browned.

5. Add the BBQ sauce and mix well.

6. Take pan off the heat and build your sandwiches.

BANG BANG CAULIFLOWER
(SERVES 8–10)

DRY MIX INGREDIENTS

- 4 cups (560 g) all-purpose flour
- 1 cup (160 g) cornstarch
- 2 tablespoons (30 ml) Cajun seasoning
- 2 tablespoons (30 ml) garlic powder
- 2 tablespoons (30 ml) onion powder

WET MIX INGREDIENTS

- 1½ cups (210 g) all-purpose flour
- 1 tablespoon (15 ml) Cajun seasoning
- 2 cups (480 ml) water

CAULIFLOWER INGREDIENTS

- 2½ cups (600 ml) canola oil
- 24 ounces (680 g) fresh cauliflower florets

SAUCE INGREDIENTS

- 4 cups (960 g) vegan mayo
- 3 tablespoons (45 ml) sriracha
- 2 cups (480 g) sweet chili sauce
- 2 tablespoons (30 ml) garlic paste

THIS IS SUPPOSED TO BE A SPICY DISH! IF YOU DON'T LIKE TOO MUCH SPICE/HEAT, USE LESS OF THE CAJUN SEASONING, SRIRACHA, AND SWEET CHILI SAUCE.

EQUIPMENT

- 3 mixing bowls
- Mixing spoon
- Medium saucepot
- Deep fry thermometer
- Tongs
- Spider for frying
- Sheet pan lined with paper towels
- Whisk

THIS KIND OF SPIDER ISN'T A CREEPY BUG! IT'S A KITCHEN TOOL USED TO REMOVE FOOD FROM HOT LIQUIDS. ITS NAME COMES FROM THE SPIDER WEB-LIKE APPEARANCE OF ITS BASKET.

INSTRUCTIONS

1. Mix all dry ingredients in one bowl and set aside.

2. Mix all wet ingredients in a separate bowl and set aside.

   PARENTAL SUPERVISION IS A MUST FROM HERE ON OUT.

3. Fill medium saucepot halfway with canola oil and heat on stove on medium until it reaches 365°F (185°C). It should get to a high enough temperature in about 10 minutes.

   NOTE: YOU WILL BREAD AND FRY THE CAULIFLOWER IN BATCHES (NOT ALL AT ONCE).

4. Take about 7 florets, dredge in dry mix, then wet mix, then again in dry mix.

5. Use tongs to place the florets in the hot oil. (Do not drop the florets from high up because it will make the oil splatter.) Cook until golden brown.

6. Use the spider to remove cauliflower from the oil and place on the sheet pan lined with paper towels. (The paper towels will absorb the excess oil.)

7. Once all frying is done, combine sauce ingredients in the third mixing bowl and whisk until smooth.

8. Toss the florets in the sauce until they're thoroughly covered.

VEGAN MAC & CHEESE

(SERVES 10–12)

INGREDIENTS

- 16 ounces (450 g) cavatappi pasta
- 1 14-ounce (400 g) pack firm tofu
- 6 ounces (170 g) raw, unsalted cashews
- 1½ teaspoons (7.5 ml) Cajun seasoning
- 1½ teaspoons (7.5 ml) garlic salt
- 1½ teaspoons (7.5 ml) onion powder
- 1½ tablespoons (22.5 ml) kosher salt
- 1½ tablespoons (22.5 ml) fresh cracked black pepper
- 1 tablespoon (15 ml) Dijon mustard
- 1 cup (120 g) shredded vegan cheddar cheese
- 1 cup (120 g) shredded vegan pepper jack cheese
- Nonstick cooking spray
- 1 cup (120 g) seasoned breadcrumbs

EQUIPMENT

- Medium saucepot
- Strainer
- Blender
- Mixing bowl
- Mixing spoon
- Large baking dish

1. Preheat oven to 425°F (220°C).

2. Cook pasta in saucepot per instructions on the box. Strain once cooked and set aside.

3. In the blender, blend tofu and cashews until smooth.

4. Combine tofu-cashew mixture with seasonings and mustard in the mixing bowl.

5. Add the cavatappi pasta and the cheese to the mixing bowl. Mix everything together.

6. Grease baking dish with nonstick cooking spray.

7. Transfer pasta to baking dish and top with breadcrumbs. Bake for 20–25 minutes.

VEGAN PRODUCTS OFTEN HAVE A DIFFERENT TASTE OR CONSISTENCY COMPARED TO NON-VEGAN PRODUCTS. THE MORE YOU MAKE THIS RECIPE, THE MORE YOU MAY WANT TO EXPERIMENT AND PUT YOUR OWN TWIST ON THE INGREDIENTS.

COCONUT GELATO

(SERVES 4-6)

INGREDIENTS

- 1 cup (240 ml) unsweetened coconut milk
- 2 cups (480 g) heavy coconut cream
- 1 cup (200 g) granulated sugar (or coconut sugar)
- 3 tablespoons (45 ml) coconut or oat milk powder
- ½ tablespoon (7.5 ml) vanilla extract or paste

EQUIPMENT

- Medium saucepan
- Whisk
- Large bowl
- Strainer
- 1-quart (960 ml) container
- Ice-cream maker

TOPPINGS

- Shredded coconut
- Dry roasted macadamia nuts
- Granola

INSTRUCTIONS

1. Combine all ingredients in a pot on low heat and whisk until sugar is dissolved. Do not bring to a boil! Strain the warm mixture into a 1-quart (960 ml) container.

2. Create an ice bath by filling the large bowl halfway with ice, then pouring water over the ice until the bowl is half-full.

3. Put the 1-quart (950 ml) container into the ice bath so it can begin to cool.

4. After 15 minutes in the ice bath, remove and dry the container. Cover the container, and place in fridge for another 1–2 hours until cold.

5. The mix is ready to put in your ice-cream maker. Follow instructions provided for the machine.

6. Serve with the shredded coconut, dry roasted macadamia nuts, granola, or any other toppings of your choice.

IF YOU DON'T HAVE AN ICE-CREAM MAKER, JUST POUR THE MIXTURE INTO POPSICLE MOLDS AFTER STEP 1. YOU CAN ALSO POUR THE MIXTURE INTO ICE CUBE TRAYS, FREEZE, AND MIX IN A BLENDER TO MAKE A VEGAN MILKSHAKE.

Glossary

A

Aioli: condiment similar to mayonnaise made from garlic and olive oil

Air fryer: small appliance for quickly cooking foods using hot air currents

B

Bake: heat food in an oven with hot, dry air at a lower temperature than roasting

Baking dish: an oven-safe container mainly used for baking casseroles or pasta dishes

Blender: electric tool that crushes ingredients or mixes them together

Boil: raise the temperature of liquid until it bubbles

Broil: cook with high, direct heat from a broiler

Broiler: the upper heating element of an oven

C

Chef's knife: versatile knife that can be used for all basic cuts

Chiffonade: finely slice leafy greens or vegetables

Combine: stir ingredients together with a spoon or a mixer on low speed

Contaminant: bacteria, parasite, or toxic substance

Cooking thermometer: instrument used to measure the internal temperature of food

Cross-contamination: transferring contaminants from one surface or substance to another

Cutting board: board on which food is cut, often made of wood, glass, plastic, or silicone

D

Dice: cut into small square pieces

Dog knife: knife sharp enough to cut through produce, but not sharp enough to pierce your skin

E **Emulsify**: combine liquids very slowly, usually drop by drop, while beating vigorously

F **Flattop griddle**: a flat surface made of stone or metal on which food is cooked
Fry: cook food with hot fat or oil

G **Garnish**: add decorative or savory elements to food
Glaze: a thin, glossy coating on food
Grate: rub food on the small holes of a grater to create small, powdery pieces
Grater: metal kitchen tool with sharp-edged holes that are used to grate or shred food

J **Julienne**: cut fruits or vegetables into matchstick-size pieces

L **Ladle**: large spoon with a deep bowl and long handle

M **Marinade**: sauce made with oil, vinegar, spices, and herbs; used to soften or add flavor to foods, especially meat or fish
Mince: finely chop foods into tiny pieces
Mix: similar to combine, but usually more thoroughly so that the individual components are no longer distinguishable
Mixing spoon: large spoon, often made of wood and sometimes featuring a hole in the center, allowing for quicker mixing

N **Nonstick**: describes a coating on a cooking surface that prevents food from sticking, sometimes applied by a spray

Oven mitts: safety gloves that allow you to properly and safely handle hot items

Parchment paper: greaseproof paper used in baking and cooking
Paring knife: small knife used for fine cuts on larger items
Peel: remove skin or rind with a knife or peeler
Preheat: bring to temperature ahead of time

Roast: cook with high heat in an oven or over a fire
Roasting pan: a large, deep pan with handles; used for cooking meat and vegetables in the oven

Sanitization: creating a clean and healthy environment for cooking that prevents cross-contamination
Saucepan: a small but deep pot with a long handle; used to cook sauces and other liquids
Saucepot: a larger version of the saucepan with taller sides
Sauté: heat food quickly in a little hot fat or oil
Sauté pan: a pan with high, straight sides and a lid
Sear: cook at a high temperature until a crust forms on the surface of the food
Seasoning: salt, herbs, or spices added to food to improve the flavor
Serrated bread knife: long, saw-like blade used to cut bread
Sheet pan: a thin, shallow pan; used for baking in the oven
Shred: rub food on the large holes of a grater to create long, thin strips
Sifter: tool that helps break up large pieces of flour, sugar, and other powdered foods

Simmer: gently cook food in a liquid at just below the boiling point

Skewers: long sticks (made of wood or metal) used to pierce and hold several small items at once to assist in cooking and turning

Skillet: a metal pan with a long handle; used for frying or sautéing

Slotted spoon: a large spoon with several holes or slots in its bowl; used to drain liquid from food

Spatula: a broad, flat, flexible utensil; used to spread, mix, and lift foods

Spider: a shallow wire basket attached to a long handle; used to lift food from hot oil or other liquid

Stockpot: a large pot with a thick base; often used to cook soup

Strainer: a large bowl with holes or slots in it; used to drain liquids from food

U

Utensil: handheld tool used in food preparation

W

Whisk: a cooking utensil with a long handle and a series of wire loops; used for whisking, whipping, or stirring

Wire rack: a utensil made of wire mesh on which foods are placed to cool

Wok: a deep, rounded pan with handles; especially used in stir-frying food

Wooden spoon: often used for cooking on the stovetop, doesn't transfer as much heat as metal utensils

About the Author

Celebrity chef and Food Network star **Darnell SuperChef Ferguson** believes that everyone has the ability to be an everyday superhero. In addition to his busy schedule hosting and guest starring in cooking shows for network television and talk shows, Darnell is a restaurateur, entrepreneur, former member of the cooking team for the 2008 Beijing Olympics, husband, father of eight, and cookbook author. During his spare time, Darnell can be found giving back to his local community and spending time with his wife and their eight kids at their home in Louisville, Kentucky.

CONGRATULATIONS, SUPERCHEF IN TRAINING! YOU'VE FINISHED THE FIRST SUPERCHEF FAMILY COOKBOOK.
NOW GO OUT THERE AND COOK UP THESE RECIPES FOR THE ONES YOU LOVE!

CERTIFICATE OF

ACHIEVEMENT

THIS CERTIFICATE IS PRESENTED TO

_____

WHO HAS EARNED THE TITLE OF

SUPERCHEF

IN TRAINING

ON THIS DATE

_____

BOOK 2 WITH
NEXT-LEVEL RECIPES
AND TECHNIQUES
COMING SOON!

Darnell Superchef Ferguson

DARNELL SUPERCHEF FERGUSON

Combine devotion time with the everyday experience of cooking and enjoying food together as a family. Make memorable experiences that will enrich every family member's life!

The Family Cookbook Devotional

50 Recipes for Faith, Food, & Fun!

amber pike

ROSEKiDZ

CP1906

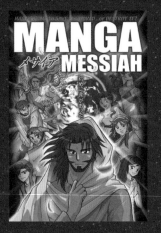
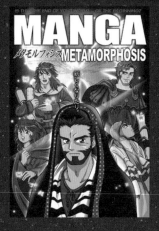